# CONSTRUCTIVISM IN FILM

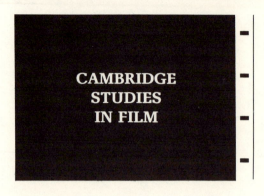

**CAMBRIDGE
STUDIES
IN FILM**

GENERAL EDITORS

Henry Breitrose, *Stanford University*
William Rothman

ADVISORY BOARD

Dudley Andrew, *University of Iowa*
Garth Jowett, *University of Texas at Houston*
Anthony Smith, *British Film Institute*
Colin Young, *National Film School*

OTHER BOOKS IN THE SERIES

Paul Clark, *Chinese Film*
Sergei Eisenstein, *Nonindifferent Nature* (trans. Herbert Marshall)
Paul Swann, *The British Documentary Film Movement, 1926–1946*

# CONSTRUCTIVISM IN FILM

*The Man with the Movie Camera*

A Cinematic Analysis

VLADA PETRIĆ

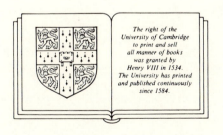

## CAMBRIDGE UNIVERSITY PRESS

CAMBRIDGE

LONDON   NEW YORK   NEW ROCHELLE

MELBOURNE   SYDNEY

Published by the Press Syndicate of the University of Cambridge
The Pitt Building, Trumpington Street, Cambridge CB2 1RP
32 East 57th Street, New York, NY 10022, USA
10 Stamford Road, Oakleigh, Melbourne 3166, Australia

First published 1987

Printed in the United States of America

*Library of Congress Cataloging-in-Publication Data*
Petrić, Vladimir.
Constructivism in film.
(Cambridge studies in film)
Filmography: p.
Includes bibliographies and index.
1. Chelovek s kinoapparatom.   2. Vertov, Dziga,
1896–1954 – Criticism and interpretation.   I. Title.
II. Series.
PN1997.C452225P48   1986   791.43'023'0924   86–12893

*British Library Cataloging-in-Publication Data*
Petrić, Vlada
Constructivism in film : The man with the
movie camera : a cinematic analysis. –
(Cambridge studies in film)
1. Vertov, Dziga – Criticism and
interpretation
I. Title
791.43'0233'0924   PN1998.A3V38


ISBN 0 521 32174 3

# Contents

**Preface**

For a brief period in its cultural history, the USSR enjoyed a unique marriage of liberal artistic expression and generous government support. Immediately following the October Revolution, Soviet artists felt free to engage in the most original and controversial of experiments, including those which clashed with the official party line. Those few years of ideological freedom and creative enthusiasm gave birth to some outstanding avant-garde achievements that still inspire artists worldwide to express themselves in ways uncompromised by artistic conventions or political dictates.

Dziga Vertov was one of the most unorthodox artists in the Soviet avant-garde movement, in both his style, exhibited by his documentary films, and his concept of cinema as a social force and as a medium for artistic expression. Inspired by constructivist and futurist ideas, Vertov saw cinema as an autonomous art and conceived of a film as a "building" made of numerous units (shots) and appropriate "architectural" procedures (shooting techniques), the meaning and impact of which were to be determined by the image composition, juxtaposition of shots, and cinematic integration of all components, including the narrative.

An inspirational force behind the group of film enthusiasts known as the *kinoks*, Vertov struggled to prove that film is a universal language of expression, intelligible to all people regardless of national borders because it is capable of constructing "sentences" and "phrases" that convey ideas more powerfully than any other means of communication. He considered the camera to be the instrument an artist could use to penetrate the essence of external reality. Identifying himself as a worker among other workers, Vertov regarded his movies as "productive objects," or "film-things," intended to help the audience – workers, peasants, and ordinary citizens – to see "through and beyond" the appearance of mundane reality. He believed that cinema as a revolutionary force could affect the mass consciousness and incite people to reject bourgeois melodramas (photoplays), which Vertov, echoing Marx, labeled "an opiate for the people." At the same time, he wanted to demonstrate the cinema's exceptional power, which could be used as an educational means to build the new society.

Vertov's most radical achievement and his masterpiece, *The Man with the Movie Camera*, is based on the constructivist concept known as "art of fact." This nonfiction (unstaged) film, as its credits specify, is "an experiment in the cinematic communication of visible events, executed without the aid of intertitles, without a script, without theater, without sets and actors." It introduces numerous innovative stylistic features through its genuine montage structure, which challenges conventional narrative movies as well as traditional documentary filmmaking. Destined as early as its first screening to be controversial in every respect, yet to make a profound mark on world cinema, Vertov's work has exerted tangible influence on such directors as Jean Rouch, Richard Leacock, Frederick Wiseman, Roberto Rossellini, Jean-Luc Godard, Satyajit Ray, Andrzej Wajda, Dušan Makavejev, Stan Brakhage, Don Pennebaker, Bruce Conner, and Jonas Mekas. Particularly intriguing is the relationship between Vertov's "Film-Eye" method and "The Camera Eye" section in Dos Passos's fiction *USA*, to whom Vertov refers in his diary. (While this book was in press, I learned of the study entitled *In Visible Light: Photography and the American Writer*, soon to be published by Oxford University Press, in which Carol Shloss dedicates an entire chapter to Vertov's influence on Dos Passos.)

A close examination of the film's key sequences reveals the structural complexity of *The Man with the Movie Camera* on both thematic and cinematic levels. The relationship between its diegetic meaning and its cinematic execution is often so intricate that one needs to view the film – or parts of it – repeatedly, and with the help of an analyst projector or editing table. Only by so elaborately scrutinizing the film's structure can one understand its complexity (just as one rereads passages of Joyce's *Ulysses* in order to appreciate its dense literary style). The use of the analyst projector is particularly necessary to detect those shots consisting of only one or a few frames that otherwise remain imperceptible, even after repeated viewings. Furthermore, the viewer is expected to be acquainted with the specific historical, political, economic, geographical, and environmental facts referred to throughout the film, all of which possess subtle ideological and psychological implications.

Chapter I outlines Vertov's position in relation to constructivism, futurism, formalism, and suprematism, the leading avant-garde movements in the Soviet Union of the 1920s. Vertov's association with the group of artists and intellectuals gathered around Mayakovsky's journal *LEF* is examined in terms of how Mayakovsky's poetic works influenced Vertov to write deconstructed stanzas and to lay out his film scripts poetically. In both endeavors he followed Mayakovsky's style as well as his practice of graphically displaying lines on the page in a collagelike style.

Although the participants in the Soviet avant-garde movement were unified by their aversion to bourgeois art, this unity did not preclude divergent tendencies within the same artistic trend, as well as conflicting attitudes among the individual artists and theorists. One such disagreement is exemplified by the dispute between Vertov and Aleksei Gan, the most militant of the constructivists, who strove for new revolutionary art and insisted on its being politically responsible to society. Even more controversial were the debates Vertov had with Sergei Eisenstein concerning the "true" nature of documentary cinema, the ideological function of montage, and the role of actors in staged (fictional) films.

With the eventual victory of socialist realism, officially proclaimed as the only "correct" approach to art, and their ensuing disappointment with the New Economic Policy (NEP), which encouraged the production of entertainment movies, Vertov and Mayakovsky realized the impossibility of fulfilling their revolutionary ideals. As the suppression of the avant-garde movement reached its peak in the early 1930s, Vertov's cinematic experimentation was proclaimed "unsuitable" and considered undeserving of support from the Ministry of Cinematography. Attacked by the orthodox film critics for being "formalistic" and therefore "inaccessible" to the masses, Vertov gradually sequestered himself from public life, while his films were removed to the state archive's vault.

Chapter II offers a thematic reading of *The Man with the Movie Camera* through in-depth examination of presented "life-facts" and their function within the thematic context, as well as the film's overall montage structure. To facilitate analysis of the sequences and individual shots, a breakdown of the film's basic themes is presented at the chapter's beginning. This segmentation emphasizes the thematic units as defined by the montage reconstruction of the recorded events.

To substantiate the ideological reading of key sequences, each analysis is accompanied by a shot-by-shot breakdown and illustrated by frame enlargements. Quotations from Vertov's theoretical writings are used to illustrate particular stylistic and theoretical features, or to justify the conclusions drawn later in this book. The "Film-Eye" method, the "Film-Truth" principle, the "Theory of Intervals," and the concept of disruptive–associative montage are discussed according to the Marxist belief in a dialectical contradiction that imbues all events in the material world. The chapter ends by systematically examining the film's different points of view, specifying their diegetic and structural functions.

Chapter III contains a formal analysis of selected sequences that best illustrate Vertov's directorial style and clearly elucidate his theoretical concepts, which are sparingly defined in his writings. Accompanied by frame enlargements and diagrams, the formal analysis shows how Vertov applied to cinema many basic constructivist principles, among them the idea that the artistic process is analogous to industrial production — hence the term "Productive Art."

In collaboration with his wife, Elizaveta Svilova (the Editor in the film), and his brother, Mikhail Kaufman (the Cameraman in the film), Vertov tried to establish cinematic equivalents of certain concepts developed by the formalist poets and suprematist painters, influences of which are most evident in those semirepresentational shots and montage sequences composed of only one or two frames, generating unique kinesthetic energy through cinematic abstraction. Vertov's most original experiments with subliminal montage grew, apparently, from his theoretical interest in the psychology of perception as well as his practical exploration of recording sound and movement, performed during his study at the Psycho-Neurological Institute in St. Petersburg.

Close structural examination of *The Man with the Movie Camera* reveals cinematic values that cannot be properly perceived nor seriously studied when the film is projected at regular speed: the most fascinating optical resolutions in this film are hidden within its complex montage structure. This fact alone suggests the extent of originality and modernism pervading Vertov's method. His last silent film marks the peak of Vertov's creative imagination, which was at odds with all facets of the traditional directorial style, every aspect of established shooting technique, and conventional editing rules. He fought uncompromisingly against the common practice of using the camera merely to record the other arts, or, equally, to register everyday events superficially.

Chapter III ends with an analysis of the three basic graphic patterns (vertical, horizontal, and circular) prevailing in most shot compositions throughout the film. Integrated by montage, these patterns attain an optical "pulsation" that — on the screen — transforms recorded "life-facts" into representationally ambiguous imagery, thus defying the spectators' customary perception of reality and its interpretation. With such remarkable cinematic features, *The Man with the Movie Camera* continues to challenge orthodox filmmaking, reject literary/theatrical theories of the medium, and demonstrate that cinema is an autonomous means of expression — "a higher mathematics of facts."

The appendixes provide necessary documentation for the three chapters and serve as reference material for the reader. They include the following:

1. the introductory statement as presented in the film's opening credits,
2. an annotated bibliography of Vertov's articles,
3. an annotated filmography of Vertov's work,
4. a biographical sketch of Vertov's career, and
5. a selected bibliography related to Vertov's work in general.

Frame enlargements (with numbers corresponding to the figures and plates marked throughout the book) are reproduced at the end as a separate section. They were realized by my assistant, Barry Strongin, who photographed the frames of a 16mm print projected on the screen by an analyst projector. Computer illustrations were drawn by Steve Eagle. The shot descriptions are quoted from the shot-by-shot breakdown executed by the author and Roberta Reeder (a copy of the complete breakdown is housed at the Harvard Film Archive). The index was compiled by Renata Jackson.

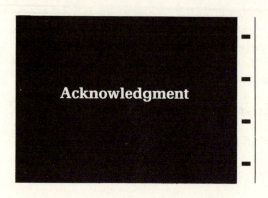

## Acknowledgment

The completion of this book would not have been possible without the assistance of many people who participated in the preliminary research, close cinematic analysis, and final literary editing of the text.

To avoid the risk of excluding any of the students, colleagues, and friends who – in one way or another – generously contributed to this endeavor (which, with few breaks, spanned almost a decade), I will, sincerely and wisely, follow Vertov's example and assign myself the role of "author-supervisor of the experiment" carried out by numerous *kinoks*.

Without the help of the *kinoks*, Vertov would not have been able to realize his projects; similarly, my goals embodied in this work would never have been accomplished without the help of those who deeply believed in it, collaborated with me, and provided encouragement when it was most necessary.

V. P.

CHAPTER

I

Dziga Vertov
and the Soviet
avant-garde movement

It is far from simple
to show the truth,
yet the truth is simple.
        – Dziga Vertov

## The *kinok*s

The decade after the October Revolution unleashed one of the most exciting periods in Russian art. Although the majority of the artists remained committed to the forms of expression dominant before the revolution, the avant-garde groups in search of ways to express the needs and goals of the newly liberated working class chose forms and subjects as innovative and experimental as the times. These revolutionary enthusiasts met a serious challenge in the attitudes of the traditional artists, as both groups strove to define theoretical concepts for the artist's role in the new Soviet state, and as numerous factions of the avant-garde adopted varying and often mutually conflicting ideological positions. The resulting differences of opinion did not, however, prevent the avant-garde artists from collectively promoting artistic experimentation and freedom of expression. This was particularly evident in cinema, which was considered the most powerful means of communication and expression.

Spurred on by avant-garde experiments taking place in other arts, Dziga Vertov envisioned the development of an unconventional cinematic mode that could be universally understood. To accomplish this he demanded that fellow filmmakers get rid of literary and theatrical conventions in order to create a new form of cinema that would engage the moviegoer's "dormant" consciousness and foster an active mental participation both during and after the screening. He proclaimed as

1

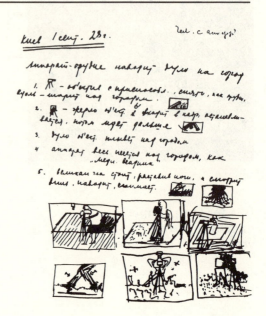

Dziga Vertov and a page from his shooting diary, dated "Kiev, 1 Sept. 28," which shows one of the shot breakdowns for *The Man with the Movie Camera*. The constructivist drawing is by I. Galadzhev.

the most urgent task the need to replace bourgeois melodramas with revolutionary newsreels reflecting everyday life. Vertov surrounded himself with a group of collaborators whom he called the *"kinoks"* [*kinoki*], a neologism that reflected their ardent dedication to film.* The members of the *kinok*s were young cameramen, editors, technicians, and animators, including Mikhail Kaufman, Vertov's brother who, in addition to playing the "protagonist," served as the cameraman for *The Man with the Movie Camera,* and Vertov's wife, Elizaveta Svilova, the film's editor, who played herself in that role.†

Vertov, Kaufman, and Svilova formed the Council of Three [*Soviet troikh*] – "the higher organ of the *kinok*s" [*visshii organ kinokov*] – which bore responsibility for the production policy of the cooperative. The *kinok*s promulgated and defended their views with idealistic zeal,

* Vertov's neologism *"kinok"* is constructed from two words: *"kino"* (film) and *"oko"* (a derivative suffix that makes an agent out of a verb). In addition, *"oko"* is an archaic word for "eye." His other, though rarely used, term for *kinok*s – *"kinoglazovtsy"* – employs the modern word for "eye" (*"glaz"*).
† Besides Vertov, Kaufman, and Svilova, the *kinok*s' group included Ivan Beliakov, cameraman; Petr Zotov, cameraman and editor; Il'ia Kopalin, editor; Alexandr Lemberg, cameraman; Boris Frantsisson, animator; and Boris Barantsievich, technician.

insisting on a sharp distinction between the traditional fictional film and the new proletarian newsreel. As a member of the Council of Three, Svilova derided the directors of entertainment films as those "who do not understand that the newsreel can also be edited, and who do not know that documentary films are more important and more exciting than photoplays with actors, because the newsreel shows life that cannot be imitated by actors."[1] She concluded her statement with a question: "If one photographs a real worker and an actor playing a worker, which is better? The impersonating actor or the real man? Unquestionably the latter!"[2] Svilova's answer clearly reflected the *kinoks*' desire to free film of the theatrical conventions it had acquired while becoming "artistic," an evolution which led cinema to become merely a recording device for the performing arts.

To promote the *unstaged film*,* the *kinoks* organized special traveling cinemas known as "agit-trains" [*agitpoezd*] and regularly visited villages without movie theaters. Their efforts were instrumental for the state's effectiveness in propagandizing new political ideas: by bringing newsreels to the peasants in distant rural areas, the *kinoks* introduced film to people who had never before seen moving pictures. The extent of the *kinoks*' activities among the peasants and workers was documented in two of Vertov's newsreels, *Instructional Steamer,* also known as *Red Star* (1920), and *The Agit-Train,* also known as *VTSIK* or *On the Bloodless Military Front* (1921). It may seem contradictory that although the workers' newsreels were made for ordinary Soviet people, the *kinoks* considered themselves members of "an international movement that marched in step with the world proletarian revolution,"[3] as they wanted their films to have a worldwide distribution. Explaining the essentials of the "Film-Eye" method, Vertov urged the newly recruited *kinoks* to use their skills in confronting the world at large and to focus on everyday life while "pushing art to the periphery of our consciousness."[4] In addition to Vertov, only Aleksei Gan and Vladimir Mayakovsky were so explicit in declaring their cosmopolitan feelings soon to be proscribed by the party as a "betrayal" of the revolution.

To understand fully how Vertov applied the constructivist concept of "making an art-object" to film, it is necessary to compare his work and his theoretical views with the achievements of other Soviet avant-garde artists, especially those whose experimentation was intended to revolutionize art. Vertov believed that the camera should not disturb the natural course of events during shooting, and therefore he advised his *kinoks* to record the "life-facts" [*zhiznennyi fakty*] "as they are" so

---

* The term "unstaged film" [*neigrovoi fil'm*], meaning a film which excludes actors, in contrast to the term "staged film" [*igrovoi fil'm*], which includes actors, has a specific ideological connotation in Vertov's theory of documentary cinema.

that, with this basis, montage could then create the "film-facts" [*kino-fakty*]. This does not mean that the "film-fact" should remain structurally unchanged through the editing process. As numerous sequences of *The Man with the Movie Camera* prove, they are built on the constructivist principle of an ideational juxtaposition of different materials to produce a more meaningful structural whole.

Vertov claimed that the *staged film* was antithetical to the spirit of the revolutionary times which required the cinema's goals be in direct political alignment with those of the new socialist reality. As a strategy for achieving this, Vertov proposed the principle of "Film-Truth" [*kino-pravda*]. Upon this basis he conceived a series of newsreels under the same title, which also alludes to the first Bolshevik daily newspaper, *Pravda* ("Truth"), founded by V. I. Lenin in 1912. From this there emerged his "Film-Eye" [*kinoglaz*] directorial method, which, according to Vertov, was capable of penetrating beneath the surface of external reality in order to show "Life-As-It-Is" [*zhizn' kak ona est'*] on the screen. By shooting "life-unawares" [*zhizn' v rasplokh*], the *kinok*s fostered an undramatized cinematic presentation of reality that was caught unawares and subsequently restructured through montage, a creative procedure Vertov believed could capture the fleeting moments of reality that otherwise escape observation. He demanded that the "*kinok*-engineer" use his or her camera as an omnipotent eye to reorganize the visible world, by revealing many processes inaccessible to the naked eye, processes made visible only through the "montage way of seeing," through the "recording of movements composed of the most complex combinations."[5]

Vertov's intention to merge the human and the mechanical eye led toward two essentially disparate goals, and inevitably produced a dialectical contradiction within the "Film-Truth" principle. In their newsreels, the *kinok*s sought both to preserve the notion of "Life-As-It-Is" and to express a new vision of reality. This contrariety was blunted by the two-pronged effect of the "Film-Eye" method which, on the one hand, dealt with "life-facts" as they appeared in external reality and, on the other, employed all available cinematic devices to recreate a new visual structure (the "film-thing"), not only phenomenologically different from its prototype but far more revealing than reality itself. On the basis of these precepts, one can conclude that Vertov's concept of truth – however concerned with "life caught unawares" – is not identical with objective truth, not even with truth as it is initially recorded on the celluloid strip.

To understand fully Vertov's significance within the worldwide avant-garde trends of the 1920s, it is not only necessary to explore how he was influenced by other unorthodox artists but also how his theories and practice inspired others. Vertov, of course, was not the sole Soviet revolutionary filmmaker who rebelled against traditional art forms, yet his works represent one of the most innovative expressions of this protest. A comparative analysis reveals that, although Vertov was influenced by futurism, suprematism, and formalism, his most experimental films incorporate various principles of the constructivist method, particularly its attitude toward the creative process.

## The constructivist tradition

The constructivists, whose ideas represent the most sophisticated aspect of the Soviet avant-garde, viewed the artist as an "engineer" whose duty was to construct "useful objects," much like a factory worker, while actively participating in the building of a new society. One of the more suitable means of artistic production was the relatively new medium of film, an art form that, given its ability to convey messages to vast audiences and its capacity to reconstruct all components of natural movement, had an immense appeal for the constructivist artists: they considered it the most powerful tool available to educate the people. In this context, film should serve a dual purpose: to assist the technological revolution and environmental transformation by replacing the bourgeois mentality with a socialist consciousness and to emancipate art by focusing on the needs and responsibilities of the emerging working class.

Perhaps the most articulate definition of constructivism was put forth in the famous "Realist Manifesto" (1922) issued by the brothers Naum Gabo and Antonin Pevsner. Representing the more aesthetic wing of this movement, they wrote that "art is the realization of our spatial perception of the world," and that the artist "constructs his work as the engineer builds his bridges and the mathematician establishes his formulas of the orbits."[6] Vertov was equally preoccupied with exploring the possibilities of cinema as the "art of imagining the movements of objects in space within a conception of a rhythmic and aesthetic whole brought in accordance with the specific properties of the photographed material as well as the inner pace of each separate element."[7] *The Man with the Movie Camera* vividly exemplifies this constructivist attitude applied to filmmaking, as its key sequences achieve a high degree of visual dynamism often by intercutting abstract shots (including black or transparent frames) within otherwise representational segments of the film. As will be documented later, Vertov's dynamic and subliminal montage was considered shocking and mischievous by most contemporary critics and filmmakers, including Sergei Eisenstein, who failed to recognize the revolutionary significance of *The Man with the Movie Camera*.

It was the futurist literary tradition in prerevolutionary Russia that stimulated the constructivists' enthusiasm for technology in the early days of the Soviet state. Admiration for machines is evident in futurist paintings by Malevich, Goncharova, and Rozanova, whereas an appreciation of pure geometrical forms is dominant in Malevich's suprematist works. This is equally true of avant-garde Russian photography and film. Vertov's youthful experiments with recording sound and motion pictures attest to his inborn fascination with machinery, its "stupendous power" and the beauty of its forms. He was so thrilled by technology that he once declared: "Our artistic vision departs from the working citizens and continues through the poetry of the machine toward a perfect electrical man.... Long live the poetry of moved and moving machines, the poetry of levers, wheels, steel wings, the metallic clamor of movement and the blinding grimace of the scorching electric current."[8] This vision is best exemplified in the camera work of Vertov and Kaufman, as their footage depicting machines and bridges are often reduced to elaborate constructions silhouetted against burning furnaces or clear sky, structures transmuted by means of montage or optical devices into graphic imagery inspired by industrial design. Vertov's enthusiasm for factories and metal constructions can also be related to the "aesthetics of the machine" as elaborated by the Italian futurists. Their manifesto, "The Futurist Cinema" (1916), proclaimed the supremacy of cinema over all other art forms and described the uniqueness of cinematic language, which, although somewhat similar, substantially differs from that of painting and photography:

Cinema is an autonomous art. Cinema must therefore never copy the stage; being essentially visual, cinema must, above all, fulfill the evolution of painting, detach itself from reality, from photography, from the graceful and solemn; it must become antigraceful, deforming, impressionistic, synthetic, dynamic, freewording.[9]

Most of these qualities can be applied directly to Vertov's work, particularly to *The Man with the Movie Camera,* in which the best sequences clearly demonstrate the distinction between still photography and the freeze-frame, animation (stop-trick) and the motion picture, the image on the film strip and the image on the screen-within-the-screen, thus acknowledging the uniqueness of the cinematic process.

The rhythms of the working man and of machines play an important role in constructivist theater, particularly in the work of the most innovative Soviet theater director, Vsevolod Meyerhold.* Inspired by the

---

* Immediately after the October Revolution, Meyerhold was among the first theater directors to offer his services to the new government; nonetheless his theater was closed in 1938, and one of the greatest revolutionary theater directors became an outcast. Only the venerable Stanislavsky befriended him, making him director of the Stanislavsky Opera Theater. But in 1939, soon after Stanislavsky died, Meyerhold was at once arrested and executed by the KGB, while his wife Zinaida Raikh was subsequently found brutally murdered in their apartment.

analytical study of time and motion related to efficiency in manufacturing operations done by Frederick Winslow Taylor, the American industrial engineer, Meyerhold developed a theory of "biomechanics," which applied the "mechanics of movement" to the stage mise-en-scène. Certain actions – such as shooting an arrow or slapping a face – were reduced to sets of elementary gestures to be, almost balletically, performed by actors in a dramatic context. A similar fascination with the rhythm of machinery and the physical motion of factory workers is manifest in Vertov's early works, the *Film-Truth* series (1922–5), as well as in his films *Forward March, Soviet!* (1926) and *One Sixth of the World* (1926). In *The Man with the Movie Camera*, the dynamic presentation and kinesthetic simulation of machines is heightened by a formal reiteration in the film's montage. Through different pictorial designs, Vertov creates a geometrical interplay of gears, pistons, rods, and wheels in horizontal and vertical movement, or he juxtaposes cars and trolleys moving horizontally against the dispersed vertical flow of milling pedestrians. Like the symbolic mise-en-scène in Meyerhold's biomechanical stage performances, various passages in *The Man with the Movie Camera* explore abstract patterns of movement in the production process; shots of stopping and starting machines, handles being pulled, levers falling, cigarettes being packaged, and ore being mined all convey the mechanical aesthetic with great expressiveness. And by comparing industrial movements with those of athletes, Vertov suggests that machines also possess an expressive visual beauty. Similarly, the motion picture apparatus is equated with the human being as it suddenly begins to "walk" on its own accord: the camera is seen from an anthropomorphic point of view.

The constructivist theater had a "deconstructing" attitude toward the organization of the dramatic performance: instead of viewing a play as an inviolable entity, the performance was considered a "product" composed of many different components the "director-engineer" must arrange according to his or her understanding of the staged event. Meyerhold, for example, often shifted scenes and acts, changing their order and breaking them into numerous shorter episodes, thereby increasing the overall tempo of the dramatic action and providing a mise-en-scène with greater visual impact. In 1922, he staged Aleksandr Ostrovsky's *The Forest,* the chronology of which he intentionally ignored, rearranging the original text according to the principle of dramatic montage. Although he hardly altered the original dialogue, the actual five acts became thirty-three episodes shuffled and demarcated with pantomime interludes to lend contrasting mood and pace. The deconstructed composition of *The Man with the Movie Camera* is based on the same constructivist as well as futurist principle of creating a nonsequential structure that reflects the essence of an urban environment and the dynamism of a technological age.*

Vertov's early concept of montage, even before 1920, drew extensively on the constructivist concept of mechanical rhythm. In 1919, he wrote that all filmmakers must treat the film footage − the recorded "life-facts" − according to their ideological views, expressing their personal attitudes toward the realities presented in the individual shots then restructured through montage. On this point, Vertov differed with most of the other Soviet futurist and constructivist artists, who insisted on the absolute dominance of "facts" in art, and sought to eliminate any subjective interpretation. Vertov was less inclined to restrict his filmmaking to such a factual approach and instead strove to achieve a balance between an authentic representation and "aesthetic" reconstruction of the external world. In doing so, he merged his "Film-Truth" principle of respecting the authenticity of each separate shot with his "Film-Eye" method, which requires a cinematic recreation of events through editing. This dialectical synthesis underlies the construction of the most dynamic sequences in *The Man with the Movie Camera,* especially the formal design of the shots (see Chapter III) and the suppression of their representational outlook by the reduced duration of their appearance on the screen. Even Lev Kuleshov, who at the beginning of his film career was strongly influenced by futurist and constructivist ideas, and who, in 1922, wrote that the "essence of film lies in its composition, as well as in the alteration of the photographed pieces/shots," that "for the organization of impressions it is not important what is shot in a given piece, but how the pieces in a film alternate with one another, how they are structured,"[10] even he complied in practice with a more orthodox concept of montage and shot composition than one might expect after reading his theoretical essays. Vertov repeatedly emphasized that theory and practice should be united: in his manifestos (often conceived as introductions to his films), he emphasized the *kinoks'* duty to prepare the audience for a novel visual experience provided by the camera's "geometrical extraction of movements"[11] from external reality.

Constructivist theory exerted considerable influence on avant-garde architecture, especially in the works of Mozes Ginsburg, the Vesnin brothers, and Vladimir Tatlin.† Concerning themselves more with

---

* For more information on Meyerhold's theory of "biomechanics" and its relationship to "Taylorism," see Edward Braun, *The Theater of Meyerhold* (New York: Drama Book Specialists, 1979).
† For more information on Russian avant-garde architecture, see Anatole Kopp, *Town and Revolution,* trans. T. Burton (New York: George Braziller, 1970). Characteristically, like all other avant-garde achievements, those architectural styles that were most revolu-

structure than with decoration, these architects sought to expose the architectonic shapes expressive of functional aspects rather than to cloak a form with columns or other structural embellishments. The most extraordinary expression of this "purism" was Tatlin's unrealized Monument to the Third International, which he proposed in 1920. This colossal structure was envisioned to be twice as tall as the Empire State Building, with certain parts designed to move during the course of a year or a month, while the uppermost cube was to complete a full rotation around its axis each day. In designing the monument, Tatlin followed the formalist concept of "baring the device" [*obnazhenie priema*] whose basic function was to make the viewer conscious of the architectural structure and the attached elements moving within its space as components unto themselves, rather than as prefabricated units creating a generically functional whole.*

Vertov's attitude toward cinema, as evidenced in *The Man with the Movie Camera,* stems from a similar commitment to the examination of the mechanisms at work within a film. In an attempt to explicate his concept of cinema as the "art of organizing the movement of objects in space," Vertov underscored not only the movement of objects before the camera through rhythmic fragmentation but also the movements of the recording apparatus itself – the movie camera. Just as Tatlin strove to convey the building's relation to the passage of time, Vertov decided to reveal the multifaceted procedure of cinematic creation to the audience by showing the camera directly recording events, and by acquainting the viewer with the processes of editing and projecting film images. Thus, the viewer's attention is shifted from the object being recorded to the actual process of recording the "life-fact," substantially increasing the spectator's awareness of the cinematic devices being employed. Whether it is lighting, montage, camera angle, fast or slow motion, freeze-frame, flicker effect, or any other technique, the manifestation of the actual filmmaking forces the viewer to acknowledge the motion picture as reconstructed reality rather than its representational reflection.

Annette Michelson points to the similarity between Vertov and two other filmmakers of the period, Jean Epstein and Laszlo Moholy-Nagy.[12] Epstein's call for "the revision of perception," as well as his

tionary at the beginning of the 1920s (especially "rational functionalism") were declared "bourgeois" at the beginning of the 1930s and replaced by the clumsy Stalinist pseudo-classical style.
* "Baring the device" [*obnazhenie priema*] is a formalist principle intended to make the perceiver aware of the expressive means unique to the given medium, and thus direct the perceiver's attention to the nonnarrative aspect of the work, its formal structure. See Viktor Shklovsky's definition in his seminal article, "Art As Device" [*Iskusstvo kako priem*], included in *Poetics: A Collection of Articles On the Theory of Poetic Language II* [*Poetika: Sbornik po teorii poeticheskogo iazyka II*] (Petrograd: 1919), pp. 101–14.

particular interest in slow motion as "a new range of dramaturgy," and Nagy's concept of the camera as a "supplement of the eye," as well as his rejection of "dramatic action," have, indeed, much in common with Vertov's theoretical views. Yet the most evident kinship between Vertov and Moholy-Nagy can be found in the structure of Nagy's 1922 film script, *Dynamics of a Metropolis,*[13] written in a typical constructivist manner. The presentation of concrete details depicting factories, buildings, and traffic in a big city, the indication of shooting angles, montage pace, and camera movement, even the graphic display of lines in Nagy's script, all this is reminiscent of Vertov's unrealized scripts cited later in this chapter.

The constructivist photomontage is based upon the principle of self-reference, and it precedes the emergence of self-referential cinema. In the early 1920s, Aleksandr Rodchenko produced extraordinary photomontage compositions with snapshots of everyday events that either he or someone else had taken and subsequently combined into new photographic structures. The freedom to deconstruct the individual photographs and reconstruct them into a new order allowed Rodchenko to go beyond the customary meanings derived from ordinary stills. *The Man with the Movie Camera* draws on the same principle: the newsreel shots are used in it as "basic material" [*osnovnoi material*] transformed through a "montage way of seeing" [*montazhnoe vizhu*] or a "concentrated seeing" [*kontsentrirovannoe vizhu*] into a new cinematic vision. But Vertov did not limit his cinematic vision to the visual aspects of reality. As a complement to the "Film-Eye" [*Kinoglaz*], he introduced the "Radio-Eye" [*Radioglaz*] method, which implies the "montage way of film-hearing" [*montazhnoe kinoslyshu*] and which acknowledges Vertov's concept of montage as a dual "cinematic organization" [*kinoorganizovanie*] of the "Film-Eye" and the "Radio-Ear" [*Radioukho*].[14]

Rodchenko's concept of photomontage relates to *The Man with the Movie Camera* in yet another important respect. Like other constructivists, Rodchenko emphasized the self-referential aspect of the photograph achieved by the dualistic relationship between the image's content and the means by which the image is constructed. He suggested that the photographer should find the most expressive viewpoint that would alert the viewer to the potential of the medium.[15] Implicit in this approach is the formalist method of "defamiliarization," which entails depiction of a familiar environment in an unusual way, thus provoking the viewer to experience an unconventional perception of the world. Inspired by Rodchenko's work as well as by similar experiments in formalist poetry, Viktor Shklovsky invented the self-referential terms "making-it-difficult" [*zatrudnenie*] and "making-it-strange" [*ostranenie*].* In his article "Art as Device," Shklovsky explains that the poetic structure should be "difficult" and "strange" in order to stimulate the reader to discover subtle and often unlikely meanings that are obscured by the convention of everyday speech.[16] In line with this principle, Rodchenko's most experimental photographs employ extreme low-angle shots of buildings, smokestacks, bridges, trees, and contrasting photographic texture, often with unusual light-ng, that would transform ordinary objects into symbolic visual signs. John Bowlt notes that it is possible "to infer that Vertov borrowed some of Rodchenko's photographic methods... [for] his extreme camera angles... in *The Man with the Movie Camera.*"[17] This observation is reiterated by Camilla Gray who links Rodchenko's "constructivist photographic method" to Vertov's film style, "for example, in the catching of movement at its height... [and] the movement of maximum drama obtained by a typically constructivist low-angled shot."[18] Vertov's films do abound with low-angle shots and graphic compositions that emphasize the architectural aspects of the photographed object and emphasize its dynamic features.

Rodchenko collaborated with Vertov on several of the *kinoks'* projects, including the production of two posters, one for the *Film-Eye* series (1924), the other for *One Sixth of the World* (1926). The two men first met while contributing to Aleksei Gan's constructivist journal *Kinofot* in 1922. It is reasonable to suspect that, as the designer of several issues of the journal *LEF*,[†] Rodchenko "showed the path of revolutionary Soviet cinema to Dziga Vertov, Lev Kuleshov, and Sergei Eisenstein," as suggested by Viktor Shklovsky.[19] In addition, Rodchenko was responsible for the eccentric graphic layout of Vertov's early manifesto, "*Kinoks*. Revolution," published in *LEF* near the end of 1923. One year earlier, Rodchenko designed the unconventional intertitles in the *Film-Truth* series, as indicated in an unsigned article on constructivism published in *LEF:*

---

* The concept of "making-it-strange" [*ostranenie*] can be related to Brecht's principle of "alienation" [*Verfremdungseffekt*]. This similarity in their theoretical attitudes supports the claim that Brecht developed his concept of alienation under the infuence of Russian formalist theory.

† LEF stands for the "Left Front of Art" [*Levii front iskusstva*]. The journal *LEF* first appeared in a series of seven issues (March 1923–August 1924), with Vladimir Mayakovsky as the editor-in-chief. The second series, consisting of twelve issues, retitled *Novyi LEF* [*The New LEF*], ran from January 1927 through December 1928. Mayakovsky continued to function as the editor-in-chief of the new series only for the first seven issues, after which Sergei Tretyakov succeeded him. Mayakovsky left the journal due to his disagreement with the group regarding the question of joining RAPP, an official organization including traditionally oriented writers, most of them ardent proponents of socialist realism. For more information about socialist realism see Marc Slonim, *Soviet Russian Literature* (New York: Oxford University Press, 1964).

Rodchenko conceived the intertitles as an intrinsic part of the film itself, designing them according to the needs of montage and the script. He introduced three new ways of using intertitles: plastering them grossly enlarged in a haphazard fashion across the screen, using contrasting styles, and animating the letters spatially, so that the written text becomes an organic part of the film instead of its deadspot.[20]

The anonymous writer of this article points to Rodchenko's innate feeling for rhythm, which is also an essential feature of Vertov's montage style. Vertov and Svilova carefully developed each sequence of *The Man with the Movie Camera* according to "its own rhythm stolen from no one...[and] through the actual movement of real things,"[21] while he and Kaufman used various shooting devices to make their shots visually dynamic and of high contrast, often emphasizing the particular graphic pattern dominating the frame.

In 1923, El Lissitzky and Ilya Ehrenburg launched the idea of "art as an object" [*iskusstvo kak veshch'*], claiming that "every organized work – whether it be a house, a poem, or a picture – is an object directed toward a particular end which is calculated not to turn people away from reality, but to summon them to make their own contributions to social life."[22] To promulgate this socioaesthetic attitude, they founded the journal *Veshch'/Gegenstand/Object* (1922) whose title indicates the international aspiration of the movement. Following the constructivist ideas in his photographic experiments, Lissitzky often depicted mechanical tools as part of the photograph's graphic design; for example, "The Constructor" (1924), his self-portrait, is composed of several superimpositions of a head, hand, and compass, symbolizing the constructivist view of the artist as engineer, while the head is surrounded by a circular shape, which suggests a unification between the mind of man and the tools he employs. In *The Man with the Movie Camera,* an almost identical conjunction between the worker and the machine is achieved by a superimposition of the smiling face of a working woman and the circular form of a rotating spindle machine. Throughout the film, circular graphic forms recur in many of Vertov's and Kaufman's shots depicting the industrial environment, communication, and city traffic. In close-ups of the camera lens and the human eye (sometimes both present at once), the circular form takes on a metaphorical meaning as it reiterates the constructivist belief that the amalgamation of human and mechanical forces can "decipher the visible world as well as the invisible."[23] With this belief, Vertov urged his *kinoks* to handle the camera as an extension of their bodies and senses (an attitude accepted by certain modern experimental filmmakers). The same attitude pervades Vertov's 1923 manifesto "*Kinoks.* Revolution" in which, identifying himself with the camera, Vertov exclaims: "I, a machine, am showing you a world, the likes of which only I can see.... My road leads toward the creation of a fresh perception of the world.... I decipher, in a new way, a world unknown to you."[24]

The unorthodox use of the camera and even more unconventional approach to montage allowed Vertov, Kaufman, and Svilova to construct what Vertov termed the "autonomous film-thing" or the "absolute vision" conveyed by every existing optical means – above all by "the camera experimenting in space and time."[25] The ultimate result of this attitude was *The Man with the Movie Camera,* a work in which Vertov integrated his "Film-Eye" method with the "Film-Truth" principle, and produced the most constructivist film in the history of cinema, an achievement – conceptually and creatively – ahead of its time.


## "Art of fact"

The *kinoks'* ideas and achievements attracted the attention of constructivist critics, most of whom hailed cinema as *the* medium of the modern age. The most militant among them was Aleksei Gan who founded the first Soviet film journal, *Kinofot* (1922), and used it as a platform for propagandizing his extreme views of cinema as a "factual" art. Appealing to the Soviet constructivist artists in his book *Constructivism* (1922), Gan contended that the first task confronting artists in the new society was "to educate the workers to accept art as an active social force, and to help them come to grips with the everyday problems that rise at every turn of the revolutionary road."* Expanding this extremely political attitude toward art, Gan wrote another essay six years later, entitled "Constructivism in Cinema," outlining the political function cinema should play in society:

Film which demonstrates real life in a documentary manner – not theatrical film playing at life – that is what the new cinematic production should be.... But it is not enough to link individual moments of episodic phenomena of life through montage. The most unexpected accidents, occurrences, and events are always connected organically with the fundamental root of social reality.... Only on this basis can one construct a vivid film of dynamic and concrete reality that substantially departs from the superficial newsreel.[26]

This proclamation led Vertov to name Gan "the first shoemaker of Russian cinema" [*pervyi sapozhnik ruskoi kinematografii*], an occupation he deemed more honest than that of an "artist of Russian cinema" [*artist russkoi kinematografii*] or of "the priests of art" [*zhretsy iskusstva*] who continued to dominate the Soviet film industry. Vertov found

* Aleksei Gan, *Constructivism* [*Konstruktivizm*] (Tver: Tver'skoe izdatel' stvo, 1923), p. 54. The book is reprinted by Edizione de la Scorpione (Milano, 1977). In addition to being the editor of the journal *Kinofot,* Gan also made a documentary film, *The Island of the Young Pioneers* [*Ostrov Pionerov,* 1924], depicting the life of juvenile deliquents [*besprizornye*] in a working youth camp.

no distinction between so-called manual and creative work: he claimed that "honest filmmakers" produce equally useful objects, "just as do carpenters [*plotniki*] and cobblers [*sapozhniki*]."[27] In contrast, he ridiculed the traditional film directors, calling them "shoeshiners" [*chistilniki sapog*] who "superficially polish" everyday reality, "overcasting the [viewer's] eyes and mind with a sweet fog."[28]

It is reflective of their shared attitudes toward graphic art and visual arrangement that the design of Gan's *Constructivism* was identical to Rodchenko's layout for Vertov's manifesto "*Kinoks*. Revolution," published one year later in *LEF* (1923). The use of varying type fonts and the boxing of important portions of the article on the page reflect a futuristic inclination toward stylistic excess, as well as a constructivist tendency to link content – in an extricable way – with visual presentation, which shapes the message of the text in its own manner. By focusing on the stylistic rendition and formal arrangement of the text, Gan strove to communicate his ideological tenets according to which artistic "products" should, above all, serve the needs of the people. The same political commitment was to be required of all socialist "workers in art," including filmmakers who where expected to produce "things" in no way exceptional or distinct from those made by factory workers. Vertov took a similar view in referring to documentary films as "film-things," which he likened to buildings, while discussing his *Film-Truth* series:

*Film-Truth* is made of material as a house is made of bricks. Using bricks, one can make an oven, the Kremlin wall, and many other things. From the filmed material [shots], one can construct different film-things. Just as one needs good bricks to make a good house, so one needs good film material to organize a good film.[29]

Vertov's equation of film shots to bricks and his comparison of the filmmaker to the mason can be seen as an expansion of Gan's idea that the photographed events must be used as "masonry" for building the new society through the reorganization of reality according to political needs and the filmmaker's ideological standpoint. Obviously, Vertov's term "film-thing" [*kinoveshch*] is different from Eisenstein's term "film-image" [*kinoobraz*], which implies not only the montage juxtaposition of the shots but primarily their pictorial execution according to the principles of the plastic arts. The "Film-Eye" method, however, is exclusively concerned with the process of montage, whereas the photographic execution (the process of capturing "life-unawares") constitutes the "Film-Truth" principle.

The publication of Gan's *Constructivism* coincided with the appearance of Vertov's most important project, the *Film-Truth* series which opened on June 5, 1922, introducing a radically new concept of newsreel production. In his 1922 article "Cinematograph and Cinema," Gan stated that the cinematograph, as a mechanical tool, had been "constantly exploited" in bourgeois society for recording theatrical events; hence, he demanded that, in the new socialist environment, it be used as a "creative vehicle for witnessing everyday life, a conscious extension of the proletarian state."[30] Only with such an ideological attitude toward the cinematographic apparatus, insisted Gan, could the filmmakers produce authentic cinema [*kinematografiya*]. In his most important essay, "Long Live the Demonstration of Everyday Life" (1923), he immediately singled out Vertov's *Film-Truth* series as a genuine demonstration of "*kinematografiya*," praising it as an exemplary cinematic expression of the constructivist worldview, objectively demonstrating the technical qualities of cinema through the "direct recording of actual socialist processes and their dynamics without the outside aid of the high-priests of absolute art." At the same time, Gan urged the *kinok*s to "construct films based on reality and, by means of montage, to extract the maximum truth from life-facts presented on the screen."[31]

Gan saw "kinematografiya" as the ideal medium to utilize what he called *tectonics* ("the essential component of the constructivist method"), which could allow artists to escape from the "dead end of traditional arts' aestheticizing professionalism," and move instead toward active artistic expression reflective of an "overall communist construction."[32] At first sight, it seems that the concept of tectonics was incongruous with the suprematist insistence on the nonobjective, abstract, and self-referential aspects of art/work and its articulation on the basis of composition, volume, interrelationship of masses, speed and direction of movement; yet, suprematists fought against the traditional roster of the arts on the same front as constructivists, repelling worn-out aesthetic concepts through elaborate and scientifically founded formal research. Gan's tectonics actually represented one of the three constructivist principles (together with "textures as forms of supply" and "construction laws as forms of surface resolution") and were directly related to the ideological context of dialectical materialism and its function in the reconstruction of society – from capitalist to communist.

Every social structure, inevitably, must have its own "constructive tectonics," and cinema is capable of playing a major role in the transition from one social order to another. In post revolutionary Russia, to achieve the type of cinema that could contribute to the ideological struggle, it was necessary, above all, to develop a new theoretical concept based on an aesthetic attitude totally different from that which governed the obsolete bourgeois film. Gan was fully aware that it was "hard to erase 'art' from the screen," because general audiences had been for centuries "mesmerized," their brains atrophied, by bourgeois photoplays. Consequently, he found Vertov's work to be in the proper spirit with the constructivist view, especially the *Film-Truth* series no. 13, in which not only the visual aspect was in accordance with "cinema of fact," but even intertitles, produced by the constructivist Rodchenko, were conceived as "objects." What follows is Gan's — obviously constructivist — interpretation of *Film-Truth* no. 13:

LENIN
All over the screen.
The screen word!
Speaking film
in cinematic language.
Titles like electric wires,
like conductors that illuminate
reality on the screen.

And all that we see in focus,
all that happens on the streets,
the squares, the windows, posters.
And we hear as they
CHEER
all, all, all

|        |  IN  | TER  |
|--------|------|------|
| TO THE | NATI | ONAL |

and proletarian
OCTOBER.
And we see airplanes and, at the
same time, watch from them the
earth below, but the earth flies
as there appear streets and houses
seen from another view, and newspa-
pers with words of comrade

Trotsky, words that have both spatial
and temporal meaning:

"We exist, but they do not recognize
us."
"We fight, and fight not to the
life, but to the death, while we
do not hide anything."
Graves in Astrakhan, shovels bury

the bodies of our heroes fallen at

---

LENIN
Vo ves' ekran.
Ekrannoe slovo!
Govoriashshii kinematograf
kinematograficheskim iazykom.
Nadpis' kak elektricheskii schnur,
kak provodnik cherez kotoryi
pitaetsia ekran svetiashcheisis
deistvenost'iu.
I my sve - vidim v fokuse,
kak zhili i kak zhivut ulitsy,
ploshchadi, vitriny, plakaty.
I slyshim kak oni
ZOVUT
vsekh, vsekh, vsekh

|   |  MI | RO |
|---|-----|----|
| K | VO  | MU |

k proletarskomu
OKTIABRIU.
I my vidim aeroplany i odnovremenno
smotrim
s nikh vniz na zemliu, a zemljia
bezhit,
nesutsia v novom plane ulitsy, doma,
gazety
i chetkaia s prostranstvennym smys-
lom i vremennym
taktom slova tovarishcha Trotskogo:

"My sushchestvuem, a oni nas ne
zamechaiut."
"My borimsia i borimsia ne na zhizn',
a na smert' i ne skrivaem nichego."

Groby v Astrakhani, lopaty zasy-
piaiushchie tela
tela nashikh pogibshchikh geroev v

| | |
|---|---|
| Kronshtadt, for a moment the banners | Kronshtate, sklonennye znamena v moment |
| are at half-mast in Minsk. We take | pogrebennii v Minske. My snimaem golovnye |
| off our hats. Moscovites, standing | ubory. Eto delaiut moskvichi na naberezhnoi |
| on the Moskva River, do the same. | Moskvy-reke. |
| Again, scores of banners and throngs | Snova znamena vrest i ljudi stremitel'no |
| of people flood into Red Square. | idut ko Krasnuiu ploshchad'. |
| | |
| A portrait of Barbolin, the worker | Portret rabochego Barbolina, ubitogo u |
| killed in 1917. | 1917 godu. |
| A placard comes closer: | Naplivaet plakard: |
| "Glory to the partisans!" | "Slava bortsam!" |
| Then a slow montage unfolds our | A dal'she razvorachivaetsia v spoko-inom montazh |
| achievements and our victories | nashie zavoevaniia, nasha pobeda i |
| and our unyielding alliance to | nashe nekolebimoe ravnenie na |
| the machine. | mashinu. |
| Yes, cinema is great stuff! | Da, velikoe delo kinematografiia! |
| Splendid is the *Film-Truth*. | Horoshaia trinadtsataia Kino-Pravda.[33] |

Gan's description of Vertov's newsreel perfectly reflects both the constructivist way of expressing ideas (note the montagelike presentation of the events seen on the screen) as well as the dynamic structure of Vertov's *Film-Truth* series (note how various events, occurring in different places, are juxtaposed on an associative principle to convey an ideological message). One can rightly assume that this literary way of conveying images as connotative signs had an inevitable influence on the formation of Soviet montage concepts. Even the graphic presentation of this and other articles in Gan's *Kinofot* were designed with a strong emphasis on the constructivist concept of typography: the meaning of words can be enhanced and expanded by the way they are designed and laid out on the page.

The Soviet film scholar Tamara Selezneva contends that Gan's struggle for "cinema of fact" played a major role in the evolution of early Soviet film theory, and that – although the relationship between Vertov and Gan was later frought with a number of disagreements regarding the function of ideology in art – "they always stuck together in their resistance to the 'threat' of narrative cinema, which they discredited as masquerading itself in the form of newsreels, particularly in the work of Eisenstein."[34] Gan's radical attitude toward art coincided with the style of Vertov's early newsreels, but soon the ideological distance between the two men became evident. Gan retained his extreme view of cinema as an aggressive political force, whereas Vertov modified the militancy of his stance, especially with respect to cinematic language, as he showed an interest in the structural and aesthetic aspects of the medium. Yet, as Selezneva points out, despite the ideological rift, Gan and Vertov continued to share a common opposition to staged films, particularly those that used nonprofessional actors. In 1923, Gan denounced fictional, narrative, illusionistic, and "fabricated art" in the most belligerent manner:

Let us release our speculative energy and transform the healthy bases of art into the field of practical construction.... We declare ourselves irreconcilable with Art since it is intrinsically linked with theology, metaphysics, and mysticism... Death to ART.[35]

Gan condemned the "enemies" of socialist art as a reactionary force that sought to aid in the evasion of reality rather than in its confrontation. "Art of fact" was to replace traditional art tainted with such escapism, which − "through film mesmerization" − paralyzed the conscious (mental) activity of its consumers. A similar fervor characterized the slogans Vertov espoused early in his career. Addressing the *kinok*s at the June 9, 1924, conference of their cooperative, Vertov exclaimed "the Babylonian tower of art will be destroyed by us."[36] From the beginning, he considered fictional movies antithetical to the development of a true "cinema of fact," and, like Gan, rejected the rearrangement of events (mise-en-scène), which, according to Vertov, reduces the film to a "surrogate of life" [*surogaty zhizni*]. True reality, he contended, should not reside in "photoplays, [which] tickle nerves, but in 'Film-Eye,' [which] helps one to see."[37] To exemplify this statement, he drew a symbolic distinction between "Petrushka" and "Life" − the former implying the artificiality of the theater, the latter representing the actual domain of cinema.* Vertov's manifesto "*Kinoks*. Revolution," which was aimed at initiating a new direction in the Goskino production company, clearly outlined similar goals for the revolutionary cinema:

> From today on, there will be no need for the
> psychological and detective drama.
> From today on, cinema will not need theatrical
> productions recorded on a film strip.
> From today on, there will be no more representation
> of Dostoevsky or Nat Pinkerton.

---

* Vertov, " 'Film-Eye' − Petrushka or Life" (1926) [*Kinoglaz − Petrushka ili zhizn'*], Articles, p. 90. This is a separate part of the article "Film-Eye," which contains several additional parts under different titles. Petrushka is a popular character in the Russian puppet theater whose name symbolizes theatrical artificiality.